J. W. (John Wilson) Bengough

The Grip Cartoons

Vols. I & II, May 1873 to May 1874

J. W. (John Wilson) Bengough

The Grip Cartoons
Vols. I & II, May 1873 to May 1874

ISBN/EAN: 9783741118913

Manufactured in Europe, USA, Canada, Australia, Japa

Cover: Foto ©Andreas Hilbeck / pixelio.de

Manufactured and distributed by brebook publishing software (www.brebook.com)

J. W. (John Wilson) Bengough

The Grip Cartoons

THE
GRIP CARTOONS

VOLS. I. & II.

May, 1873, to May, 1874.

WITH NOTES AND INTRODUCTION

BY J. W BENGOUGH.

TORONTO:
ROGERS & LARMINIE, 22 ADELAIDE STREET EAST.
1875.

Entered according to the Act of the Parliament of Canada, in the year one thousand eight hundred and seventy-five, by ROGERS & LARMINIE, *in the office of the Minister of Agriculture.*

INTRODUCTORY NOTE.

HERE, O Public! here they are! You have been clamoring in the most importunate and flattering fashion for a re-issue of the Cartoons of *Grip*, and out of pure good humour, I have gone to work and *re-drawn* them for you, because, you must know, these destiny-shaping pictures were not originally engraved upon wood, but were produced by lithography, and in due time each was utterly erased from the stone to make way for bill-heads and cigar labels. This has been no light task, but of course my good will towards men, together with the anticipation of being an author and writing an "introduction," made it a labour of love. Now, the fact of the public request aforesaid will spare me the usual editorial humiliation of an introductory apology; and I need say nothing here about the subject matter of the sketches, as I have written an explanatory note (comprehensive and lucid enough I hope) opposite to each, and, therefore, my prefatory remarks are complete—with, by the way, a word to the Critics. Dear Critics, I defy you to do your worst. This work, as you know in your heart of hearts, is above criticism. There are no errata to be found in the text, and no false perspective or other defects in the drawings. If you hit upon anything that may persuade you to the contrary pray don't write it. Come and see me personally at No. 2 Toronto Street, where I have hung my basket, and every Saturday croak "Never Say Die" to an ever increasing circle of patrons. But what an ungrateful rook I am to be sure, thus impudently chattering to those who have shown me nothing but generosity during my career, and to be thus boring the generous Canadian Public who have, with unexampled goodness, bestowed their favours on

Their humble Raven,

𝔊rip.

CONTENTS.

Canada's Farewell to Punshon,...	1
After the Session; or, The Situation,	2
The New Mother Hubbard,	3
Law and Justice,	4
The Huntington Business,	5
An Overworked Mayor,	6
Canada's "Laocoon,"	7
Will he come to Grief?	8
Dufferin's Tormentors, or "Per vias Rectas,"	9
Isn't that a Dainty Dish to set before a King?	10
Whither are we Drifting?	11
The Beauties of a Royal Commission,	12
Waiting for Huntington,	13
Wanted, a Good Stout Boy,	14
The Irrepressible Showman,	15
Blackwash and Whitewash,...	16
"We in Canada seem to have lost all idea of Justice, Honour and Integrity,"	17
"Progressing Favourably,"	18
Rehearsing for the 23rd instant,	19
"Will he get through?"	20
A case of *Riel* Distress,...	21
"Of comfort no man speak. Let's talk of graves, and worms and epitaphs,"	22
Miss Canada's School,	23
The Political Mother Hubbard,	24
The Irrepressible Jack,	25
The Premier's Model,	26
The Liberal Programme, or the Era of Purification,	27
The Political Giant Killer,	28
The West Toronto Run	29

CONTENTS.

"Christmas Pie,"	30
Johnny's "Turn," or New Year's Joy,...	31
The Cruel Object of "Dissolution,"	32
"Never Out,"	33
The New "Heathen Chinee,"	34
Political Pastimes, ...	35
Pity the Dominie! or Johnny's Return, ...	36
Grip's Valentine to Canada, ...	37
The New Departure,...	38
The Curse of Canada, ...	39
The Opposition Quartette, ...	40
The Political Handy Andy, ...	41
A Question for Pay Day, ...	42
Grip's Perpetual Comedy, ...	43
The Vacant Chair, ...	44
The Science of Cheek, ...	45
A Touching Appeal, ...	46
Protestantism at Ottawa, ...	47
Mrs. Gamp's Home-Thrust, ...	48
The Political Atlas, ...	49
Pacific Pastimes; or, "The Hard Road to Travel,"	50
"Dignity" without "Impudence,"	51
Ambition's Thorny Path, ...	52

"NEVER SAY DIE."

No. 1.

"*Canada's Farewell to Punshon.*"

THE departure of Rev. W. MORLEY PUNSHON for England, after a few years' sojourn in Canada as President of the Wesleyan Conference, took place on the 24th of May, 1873, (the day on which the first number of *Grip* appeared.)

MAY 24th, 1873.

CANADA'S FAREWELL TO PUNSHON.

CANADA—GOOD BYE THEN, DOCTOR, AND REMEMBER ME KINDLY TO THE OLD FOLKS AT HOME.

No. 2.

"*After the Session.*"

ON the 2nd April, 1873, Hon L. S. Huntington, member for Shefford, from his place in the House, charged Sir John A. Macdonald, Premier of the Conservative Government, with having corruptly sold to Sir Hugh Allan, of Montreal, the Charter of the proposed Canadian Pacific Railway, for a large sum of money, which had been used as a Ministerial Bribery Fund in the preceding General Election. Shortly after this, and before any decided inquiry had been made into the matter, Parliament was adjourned (on May 23rd,) until the following 13th of August. The Cartoon playfully suggests the feeling of the Opposition, (represented by Hon. A. Mackenzie,) towards the accused ministry during the "vacation."

MAY 31, 1873.

AFTER THE SESSION; OR, 'THE SITUATION.'

J. A. M—c—d—n—ld.—"Come on, Old Fellow, it's all right, you know; it's My turn to Treat!"
A. M—k—n—ze.—"Oh, aye, Joney! but ye maun recollec' I'm Te-total—more especially till August!"

No. 3.

"The New Mother Hubbard."

AN allusion to the City By-Law, introduced by Alderman WILLIAM THOMSON, compelling all owners of dogs to obtain Metallic Checks certifying that the City Dog Tax had been paid.

JUNE 14th, 1873.

THE NEW MOTHER HUBBARD.

SHE WENT TO HEAD-QUARTERS AND BOUGHT HIM A CHECK,
AND WHEN SHE CAME BACK, PUT IT ON THE DOG'S NECK.
—*NURSERY RHYME.*

No. 4.

"*Law and Justice.*"

THE advisability of removing the bronze statue of the Queen from the Park had been under discussion in the City Council, and created considerable interest. *Grip*, in this Cartoon, took the liberty of suggesting a work of art to supply the place of Mr. Marshall Wood's figure. The persons represented are, in the centre, Mr. A. Macnab, Police Magistrate of Toronto; on the right, Mr. Nudell, a popular Court official; and on the left, Alderman John Baxter, J.P.

JUNE 21st, 1873.

LAW AND JUSTICE.

A DESIGN RESPECTFULLY SUBMITTED TO THE QUEEN'S PARK STATUE COMMITTEE.

No. 5.

"The Huntington Business."

"SIR JOHN courts enquiry" was the oft-repeated assertion of the Conservative newspapers, in view of the approaching session of Parliament at which the charge brought by Mr. Huntington was to be regularly tried. The Cartoon was meant to depict the gallant Knight in his "courtship" in such a way as to render the quoted statement "sorter Ironikal" as A. Ward would say.

JULY, 5, 1873.

THE HUNTINGDON BUSINESS.

"SIR JOHN *COURTS'* ENQUIRY."—The *MAIL*.

No. 6.

"*The Overworked Ma(yo)re.*

A PALPABLE and surely a pardonable pun, seeing that its object was to pay a tribute to the official industry of the Civic Chief Magistrate for 1873—Alex. Manning, Esq. A branch of the Society of the Prevention of Cruelty, &c., had been established in the City shortly before the date of the cartoon.

JULY 12th, 1873.

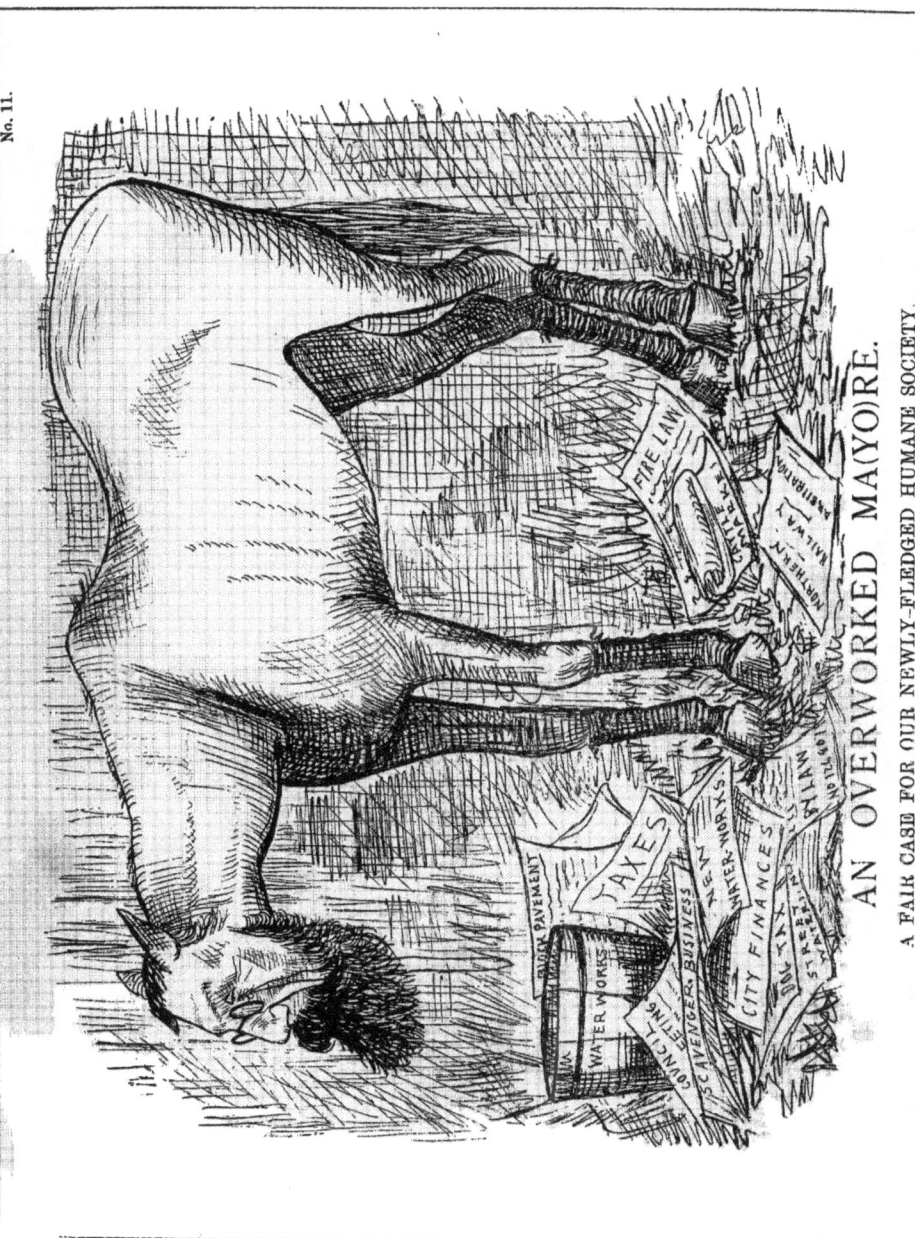

AN OVERWORKED MA(YO)RE.

A FAIR CASE FOR OUR NEWLY-FLEDGED HUMANE SOCIETY.

No. 7.

"*Canada's Laocoon.*"

An adaptation of the classical story of Laocoon and the serpents to the circumstances of some of the parties to what was already known as the "Pacific Scandal." The persons represented are Sir Hugh Allan (to whom the charter was sold), Sir John Macdonald (by whom ditto), and Sir Francis Hincks. It is due to the latter gentleman to point out that, as indicated in the cartoon, he was merely *suspected* of complicity in the matter, and most emphatically denied the truth of the allegation of his guilt, made in some of the newspapers.

July 19th, 1873.

CANADA'S "LAOCOON:"

OR, VIRGIL ON THE POLITICAL SITUATION.

"Ecce autem gemini a Tenedo, tranquilla per alta, &c."— ÆNEID, BOOK II

(Freely Translated)

When lo! two snakes (perhaps from the Yankee shore),
Together trail their folds across the floor,
With precious scandals reared in front they wind,

Charge after charge, in long drawn length behind!
While opposition benches cheer the while,
And John A. smiles a very ghastly smile !—and—
        Everybody knows the rest."

No. 8.

"Will he come to Grief?"

THE legend of this cartoon sufficiently explains its import. The facetious occupation of the Clown had its analogue in the course pursued by *The Globe* during the "Scandal" excitement—an eager and justifiable desire to see the hero of the business unseated.

JULY 26th, 1873

WILL HE COME TO GRIEF?

THE THRILLING ACT NOW IN THE RING OF THE POLITICAL CIRCUS.

No. 9.

"*Dufferin's Tormentors.*"

THE Ministerial party in the House, headed by Sir John Macdonald were exceedingly anxious for a prorogation of Parliament, the Opposition as earnestly opposed that course. Their counter entreaties to the Governor-General on the subject suggested the familiar scene of the railway passenger and his friends the "cabbies."

AUGUST 2nd, 1873.

DUFFERIN'S TORMENTORS, or *PER VIAS RECTAS.*"

J—N A. (*ANXIOUSLY.*) "CARRIAGE, SIR? 'MINISTERIAL' HOTEL—ONLY CONSTITUTIONAL PLACE IN THE CITY—COME ALONG WITH ME, SIR."

Mc—K—NZ— (*EAGERLY.*) "THIS WAY MY LORD—'REFORM' HOUSE! TAK' THE RIGHT COURSE—GIE US YER CHECKS!!"

L—D D—FF—N.—"MUCH OBLIGED, GENTLEMEN, I ASSURE YOU; BUT I HAVE A 'RIG' OF MY OWN AT HAND, YOU KNOW."

No. 10.

"*The Dainty Dish.*"

A NOTE here is perhaps superfluous. The faces of the "blackbirds" in the "pie" are those of Hon. M. Langevin (a prominent member of the Macdonald government), Sir Hugh Allan, Jas. A. Beaty, Esq. (to represent *The Leader*), Sir John A. Macdonald, Sir Francis Hincks, "Uncle Sam," and T. C. Patteson, Esq. (representing *The Mail* newspaper.) On Messrs. Blake and Mackenzie devolved the task of presenting the savoury dish before Parliament.

AUGUST 9th, 1873.

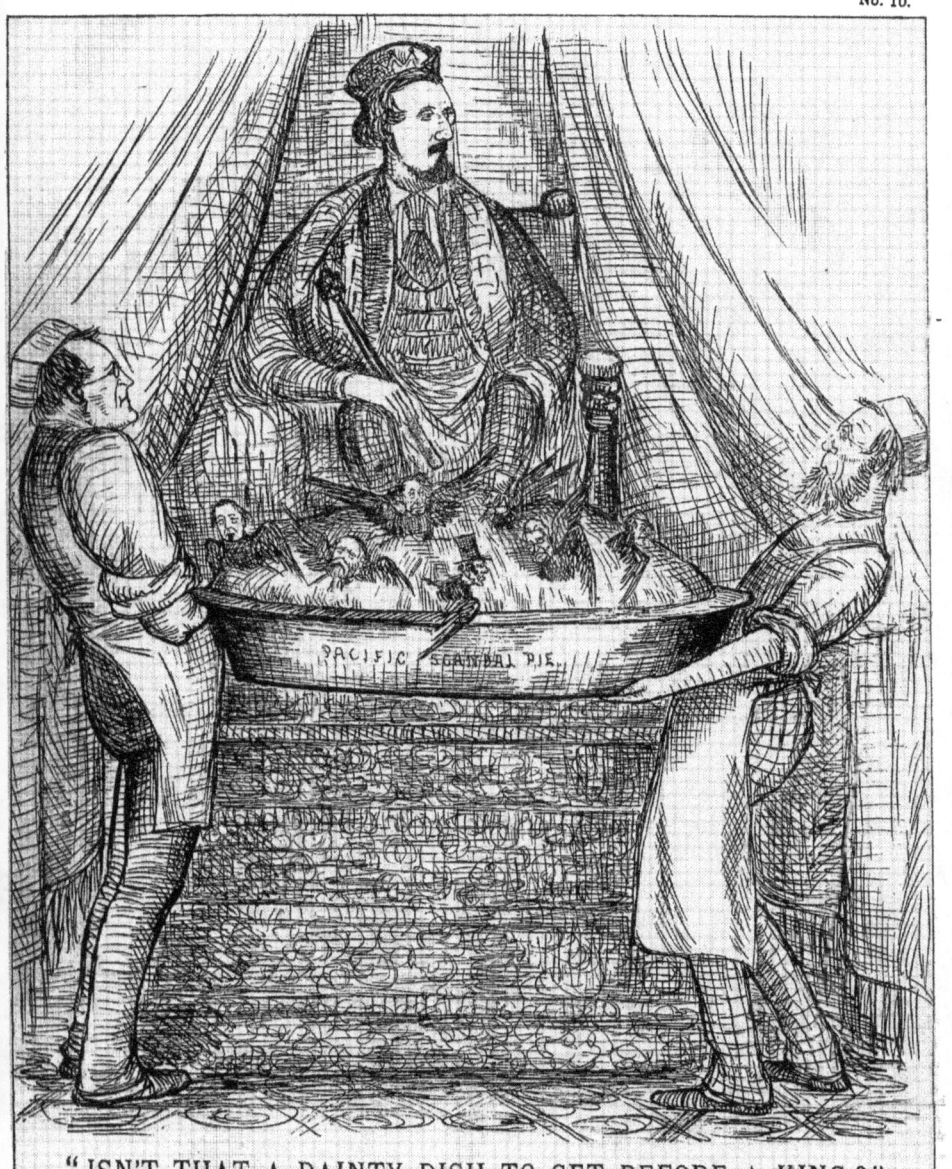

"ISN'T THAT A DAINTY DISH TO SET BEFORE A KING?"
—*Nursery Rhyme.*

No. 11.

"*Whither are we Drifting?*"

GENERAL indignation was expressed throughout the country, when, in accordance with the advice of the implicated Premier, Parliament was prorogued and the investigation of the Scandal thus delayed. The words imputed to Sir John in the cartoon had been used by him on the floor of the House, and became a popular by-word while the discussion on the subject lasted.

AUGUST 16th, 1873.

WHITHER ARE WE DRIFTING?

No. 12.

"*The Beauties of a Royal Commission.*"

THIS CARTOON was intended to satirize the appointment by Sir John A. Macdonald of a Royal Commission, absolutely under his own control, to enquire into and report upon the charges brought by the Hon. Mr. Huntington. The sentiment of the Press and public with regard to this proceeding justified the implication of the caricature, that the accused Premier was virtually "trying himself."

AUGUST 23rd, 1873.

THE BEAUTIES OF A ROYAL COMMISSION.
"WHEN SHALL WE THREE MEET AGAIN?"

No. 13.

"*Waiting for Huntington.*"

Hon. Mr. Huntington refused to acknowledge the Royal Commission appointed by the accused Minister, and declined to submit his case before it. The motive imputed to him by the Conservative Press for this refusal was fear, and in the eyes of his partizans Sir John sustained the attitude represented in the Cartoon.

August 30th, 1873.

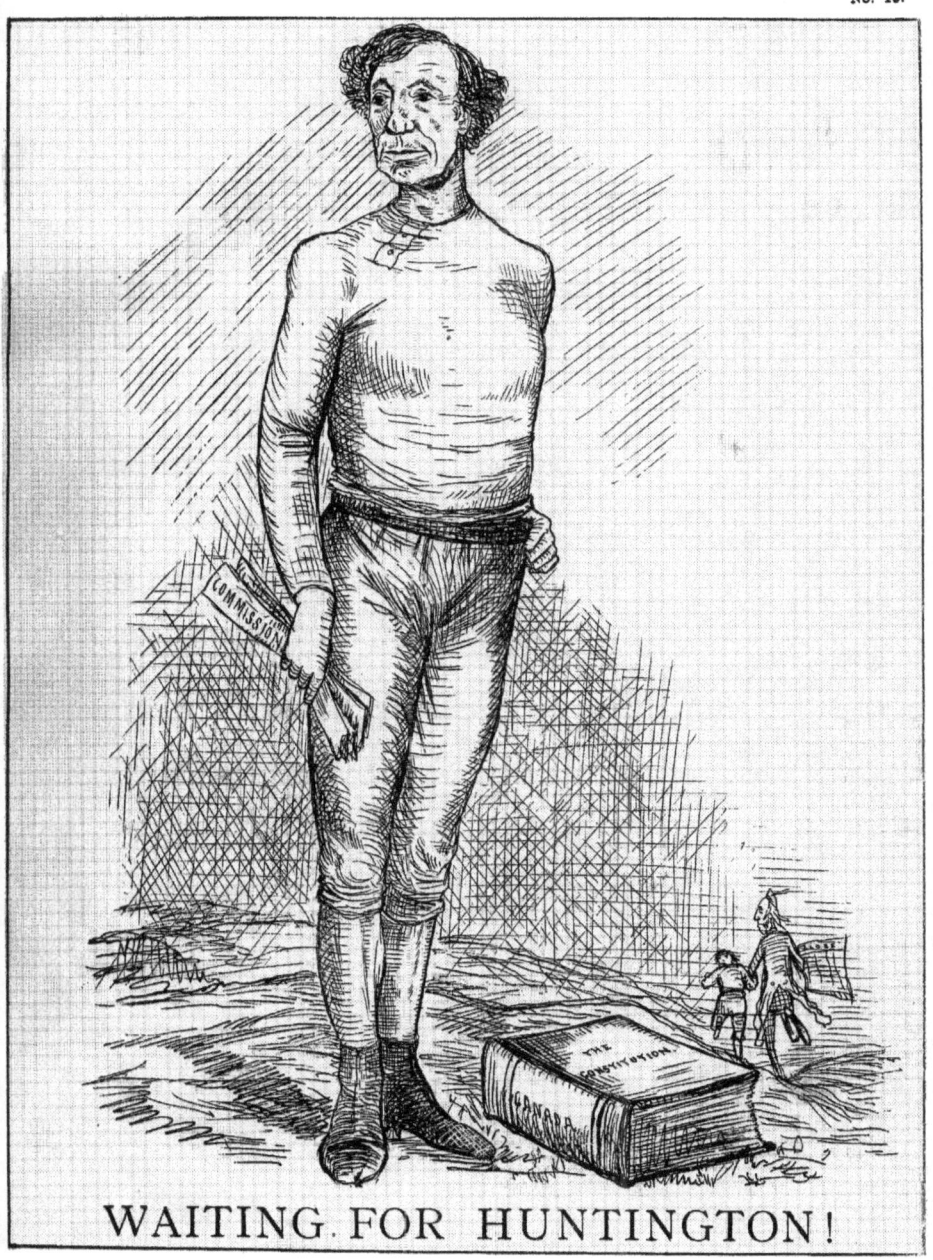

WAITING FOR HUNTINGTON!

No. 14.

"Wanted, a Good Stout Boy."

THERE were those, of course, who saw an evidence of weakness in the Governor-General's use of his prerogative of prorogation in accordance with the advice of the accused Ministers. But perhaps a "stouter boy" would have done little better in that difficult and delicate case, and certainly few "boys" could have done the work of the "place" generally so as to secure more of the peoples' respect and admiration than Lord Dufferin enjoys.

SEPTEMBER 6th, 1873.

"WANTED, A GOOD STOUT BOY."

CANADA TO BRITANNIA.—"IT WAS KIND OF YOU TO SEND HIM OVER, MOTHER; HE'S A *GOOD* BOY ENOUGH, BUT HE'S TOO *LIGHT* FOR THE 'PLACE'!"

No. 15.

"*The Irrepressible Showman.*"

APROPOS of the visit to Canada of Barnum, the Showman, during the Pacific Scandal "fever."

SEPTEMBER 13th, 1873.

THE IRREPRESSIBLE SHOWMAN.

BARNUM WANTS TO BUY THE "PACIFIC SCANDAL."

No. 16.

"*Blackwash and Whitewash.*"

"ILLUSTRATING," as the legend goes on to say, "the recent great opposition speeches, and the doings of the jolly Royal Commission." The Reformers, of course, lost no opportunity of painting Sir John in grimy colours; while it was generally acknowledged that the Royal Commissioners and the Conservative press did little more during the excitement than "whitewash" him.

SEPTEMBER 20th, 1873.

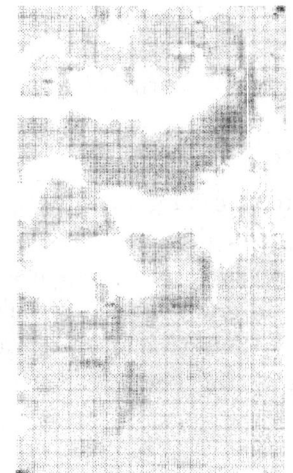

BLACKWASH AND WHITEWASH.

ILLUSTRATING THE RECENT GREAT OPPOSITION SPEECHES, AND THE DOINGS OF THE JOLLY ROYAL COMMISSION.

No. 17.

"We in Canada seem to have lost all idea of justice, honour and integrity."

So SAID the *Mail*, the leading Conservative organ, on September 26th. *Grip* sought to point this lugubrious confession with an illustration drawn from the topic of the hour.

SEPTEMBER 27th, 1873.

"WE IN CANADA SEEM TO HAVE LOST ALL IDEA OF JUSTICE, HONOUR, AND INTEGRITY."—*The* "*MAIL*," 26th Sept.

No. 18.

"*Progressing Favourably.*"

A PEEP into the hearts of the Reform Leaders during the interesting period of Sir John Macdonald's political "indisposition." The "Poor Dear Premier" may be seen, if the reader will take the trouble to peer into the bed-room.

OCTOBER 4th, 1873.

"PROGRESSING FAVOURABLY."

Miss Canada—(*anxiously*)—"DOCTORS, HOW DO YOU FIND THE POOR DEAR PREMIER?"
Dr. B—n (*for the M.D.'s*)—"MADAM, WE'VE JUST HAD A CONSULTATION; THE SYMPTOMS ARE HOPEFUL—WE BELIEVE HE CAN'T SURVIVE OCTOBER!"

No. 19.

"Rehearsing for the 23 rd."

Representing the spirit in which the Leaders of the Respective Parties approached what was expected to be the decisive date.

October, 11th, 1873.

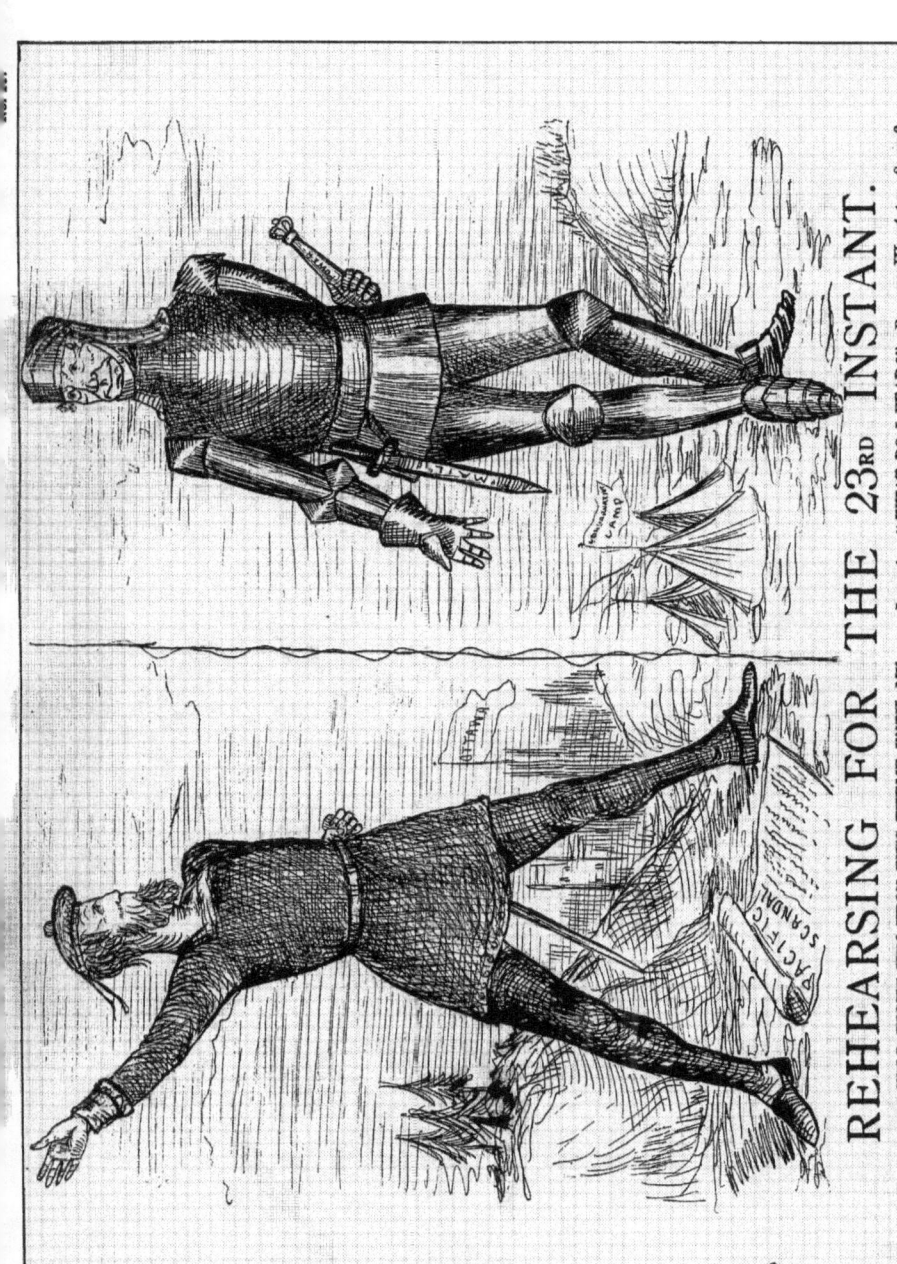

REHEARSING FOR THE 23RD INSTANT.

M—R—IE.—"I WILL FIGHT HIM UPON THIS THEME UNTIL MY EYELIDS WILL NO LONGER WAG!"—HAMLET, Act v., Scene 1.

JOHN A.—"WHAT DO I FEAR?"—RICHARD III., Act v., Scene 3.

No. 20.

"Will he get Through?"

THE question which was on all lips during the interim between the prorogation of the House of Commons on the 13th of August and the day fixed for its re-assembling, October 23rd. The prophecy conveyed in the unreasonable smallness of the hoop in the clown's hand, was duly realized.

OCTOBER 18th, 1873.

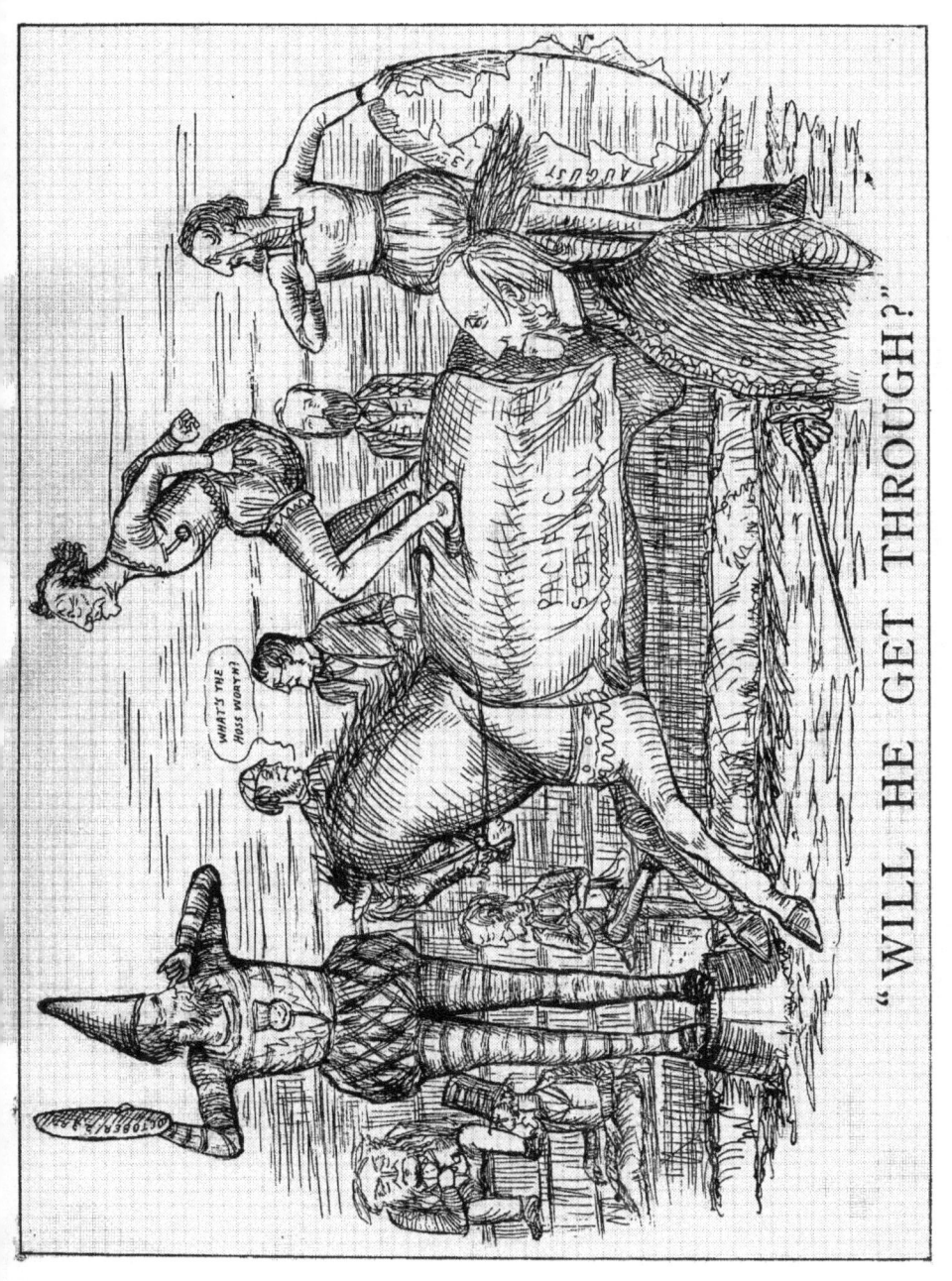

No. 21.

"*A Case of Riel Distress.*"

THE murder of Thomas Scott, at Fort Garry, during the Red River Rebellion, naturally excited great indignation throughout the Dominion, and a universal demand was made for the apprehension and punishment of Louis Riel, the leader of the malcontents, at whose instigation the deed was committed. This righteous sentiment, however, ultimately resolved itself into mere political "claptrap," and the action of the Conservative Government, then in power, was hypocritical throughout, they having secretly promised the rebels an amnesty, while publicly professing an anxious desire to "catch him."

OCTOBER 25TH, 1873.

A CASE OF RIEL DISTRESS!

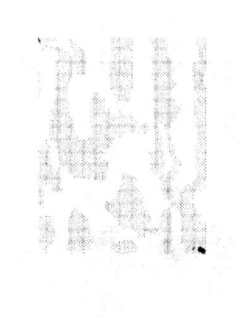

No. 22.

"Of comfort no man speak;
Let's talk of graves and worms and epitaphs!"—SHAKESPEARE.

TYPICAL of the overwhelming grief which seized the Conservative Party on being turned out of office, after a reign of nearly twenty years.

NOVEMBER 1st, 1873.

"OF COMFORT NO MAN SPEAK;
LET'S TALK OF GRAVES AND WORMS AND EPITAPHS!"—Shakespeare.

No. 23.

"*Miss Canada's School.*"

BEING a word of advice to the new Premier. The persons represented in the cartoon, are, commencing at the head of the "class," Hon. A. Mackenzie, Hon. Edward Blake, Hon. Geo. Brown, Hon. E. B. Wood, Louis Riel (who had been elected M. P. for Provencher, Manitoba), Hon. M. Langevin, James Beaty, Esq., M. P., T. C. Patteson, Esq., manager of *The Mail*, Sir Francis Hincks, and Sir John Macdonald. Monitor, His Excellency, Earl Dufferin, Gov. General.

NOVEMBER 8th, 1873.

MISS CANADA'S SCHOOL. (Dedicated to the New Premier.)

Miss Canada (*to the Boy at the Head*)—"Now Alexander, be very careful, or I'll put you where John is!"

No. 24.

"*The Political Mother Hubbard.*"

It had been currently reported in the newspapers that the dignity of the Lieut. Governorship of Ontario was to have been bestowed on the Hon. George Brown, immediately on the accession to power of the Reform Government. The new ministers discovered, however, that Sir John Macdonald, had, in the last gasp of his official life, appointed one of his own colleagues, (the Hon. John Crawford) to the position in question, besides disposing of ninety-nine other "places" in the gift of the First Minister.

November 15th, 1873.

THE POLITICAL MOTHER HUBBARD
AND JOHN A.'S "DYING INIQUITY."

No. 25.

"*The Irrepressible Jack.*"

THE circumstance under which Sir John Macdonald was deposed from power seemed to warrant the assumption of the Reformers that he was "done for." But on the contrary it only seemed the signal for additional honours to be heaped upon him by the Conservative Party, who unhesitatingly chose him leader of the opposition, and nominated him as member for Kingston, West Toronto, &c., not to mention banquets, and other species of emphasis.

NOVEMBER 22nd, 1873.

THE IRREPRESSIBLE JACK;
OR, THE CONSERVATIVE RESUSCITATION.

JOHN A. (*Side Showman*)—" DID YOU THINK THE LITTLE FELLER'S SPRING WAS BROKE, MY DEARS ?"

No. 26.

"The Premier's Model.

IN an address to the electors of Lambton, soon after the accession to power of the Reform Party, Mr. Mackenzie declared the cardinal points of the policy he would inaugurate, as leader, to be "Electoral Purity" and "the Independence of Parliament." (Before entering political life, Mr. Mackenzie followed the vocation of stone-mason.)

NOVEMBER 29th, 1873.

THE PREMIER'S MODEL;
OR, "IMPLEMENTS TO THOSE WHO CAN USE THEM."

CANADA—WELL AND BRAVELY DONE, MACKENZIE, NOW STAND BY THAT POLICY, AND I'll WITH YOU ALWAYS!"

No. 27.

"*The Liberal Programme.*"

An adaptation of one of Leech's Cartoons, in *Punch*, to Canadian circumstances----the cleansing of the Legislature after the corrupt Conservative regime.

December 6th, 1873.

THE LIBERAL PROGRAMME;
OR, THE ERA OF PURIFICATION.

No. 28.

"The Political Giant-killer."

The "Canada First" movement, having for its object the cultivation of a national sentiment and the extinction of political party strife, was inaugurated about this time.

December 13th, 1873.

THE POLITICAL GIANT-KILLER;
OR, "CANADA FIRST."

No. 29.

"The West Toronto Run."

In the General Election which followed the defeat of the Conservative Government, Mr. E. O. Bickford contested West Toronto in the interest of the New Opposition, and rested his claims to the seat mainly on the prestige of Sir John Macdonald, declaring that, if elected, he would follow that honourable gentleman through weal or woe. As the cartoon suggests, he met with defeat.

December 20, 1873.

THE WEST TORONTO RUN.

B—CKS—ND (*Jockey of the Nag "John A."*).—SAY, GUV'NOR, LOOK HERE, THIS HOSS AIN'T WOTH SHUCKS ON HIS OWN MERITS!

No. 30.

"Christmas Pie."

The treat which Santa Claus had in store for the Reformers.

December 27th, 1873.

No. 31.

Johnny's "Turn;" or, New Year's Joy.

THE election of Mr. D'Arcy Boulton as Conservative Member for South Simcoe, in the Ontario Legislature, took place about this time. Although the influence of this event on the fortunes of the late Premier of the Dominion was hardly discoverable, it was hailed by the Conservative Press as the earnest of a reaction in favour of that party. A Mr. Saunders (whose face our artist had not seen) was Mr. Boulton's opponent in the contest.

January 3rd, 1874.

No. 32.

"*The Cruel Object of Dissolution.*"

MR. MACKENZIE and his colleagues advised the dissolution of Parliament on taking office. This accordingly carried out, with the object, as the cartoon suggests, of keeping Sir John and his comrades "out in the cold."

January 10th, 1874.

THE CRUEL OBJECT OF "DISSOLUTION."

No. 33.

"*Never Out!*"

A BILL for the incorporation of the Orange Societies was at this time occupying the attention of the Ontario Legislature, and creating considerable interest. It was treated as a test question when it came to the vote, and the Opposition anticipated the defeat of the Government, who, by the way, opposed the measure. The decision of the umpire, after the ball was bowled, is pictured in the cartoon.

January 17th, 1874.

"NEVER OUT."

No. 34.

"*The New Heathen Chinee.*"

THE analogy sought to be pointed out between the new Premier and Bret Harte's famous "Ah Sin" was merely in the possession of a great advantage in the way of cards. Mr. Mackenzie went to the country with the "Pacific Scandal" for a text, and it proved as ruinous to the Conservative Party as Ah Sin's "twenty-four packs" did to "Bill Nye" and his Pardner. This explanation is needed, as the cartoon was considered, by some who misunderstood it, to impugn the honesty of the gentleman represented.

January 24th, 1874.

THE NEW "HEATHEN CHINEE;"
OR, THE WINNING HAND AND SLEEVE.

No. 35.

"Political Pastimes."

POLITICAL sport, analogous to this, occupied the minds of the "boys" and the newspapers during the recess.

January 31st, 1874.

POLITICAL PASTIMES.

No. 33.

"*Pity the Dominie; or, Johnny's Return.*"

ANENT the re-election of Sir John A. Macdonald as member for Kingston, in the general election which followed the accession of the Reform Government.

February 7th, 1874.

PITY THE DOMINIE! OR JOHNNY'S RETURN.

Canada—"HERE'S OUR JOHNNY FOR YOU AGAIN, MR. MACKENZIE! YOU'LL FIND HIM APT ENOUGH, BUT FRANKLY, SIR, HE'S FULL OF MISCHIEF!"

No. 37.

"*Grip's* Valentine to Canada."

THE leading English and American Newspapers had been interested spectators of the great Political Drama of the Pacific Scandal, and joined in praising the purity and pluck exhibited by the Canadian people in so promptly ejecting its authors from the high places they had dishonoured.

February 14th, 1874.

"GRIP'S" VALENTINE TO CANADA.

⁎ FOR INTERPRETATION WHEREOF SEE THE ENGLISH AND AMERICAN NEWSPAPERS.

No. 38.

"*The New Departure.*"

Hon. Edward Blake's withdrawal from the new Government very shortly after it had taken possession of the Treasury Benches, created an unpleasant sensation throughout the country. The hon. gentleman had been perhaps the main instrument in bringing about the fall of the preceding Cabinet.

February 21st, 1874.

THE NEW DEPARTURE.

Spouse B——E.—"FAREWELL FOR THE PRESENT, DEAR; YOU AND THE GIRLS MUST MANAGE THE HOUSE IN MY ABSENCE!"

No. 39.

"*The Curse of Canada.*"

WHISKEY.

February 28th, 1874.

out

No. 40.

"*The Opposition Quartette.*"

THE most prominent members of the Opposition (Conservative) in the Ontario Legislature were Messrs. M. C. Cameron, Q.C., J. Chas. Rykert, A. W. Lauder and A. Boultbee. These gentlemen were always most active and energetic in their labour of fault-finding, and at the time of the Cartoon were ringing the changes on the public accounts of the Province, which were undergoing examination in Committee.

March 7th, 1874.

THE OPPOSITION QUARTETTE

PERFORMING THE NEW AND HIGHLY AGGRAVATING AIR ENTITLED "PUBLIC ACCOUNTS."

No. 41.

"The Political Handy Andy."

Hon. Archibald McKellar, Commissioner of Agriculture for Ontario, whose official record was certainly marked by occasional "blunders," was, notwithstanding, popularly looked upon as one of the most trustworthy and useful members of the Mowat Ministry.

March 14th, 1874.

THE POLITICAL HANDY ANDY.

SQUIRE MOWAT.--(Per *The St. Catharines Times*, Ministerial)--"FOR SOME REASON OR OTHER YOU ARE CONSTANTLY MAKING SMALL AND FOOLISH MISTAKES!"

No. 42.

"*A Question for Pay Day.*"

THE "Opposition Quartette" had vigorously assailed the action of the Hon. A. McKellar for having, in his capacity as Minister of Public Works, granted a half holiday (at the public expense) to the workmen engaged in building the Central Prison at Toronto, to allow them an opportunity of attending a nomination meeting in the West Division of the city. In view of the meagre amount of work done on the left side of the Speaker during the Session, "Grip's" question was quite logical.

March 21st, 1874.

A QUESTION FOR PAY DAY;
Or, "CENTRAL PRISON" LOGIC APPLIED.

GRIP (loq.)—"GENTLEMEN, IS THERE ANY 'SCANDAL' ABOUT YOUR DRAWING A FULL SESSION'S PAY FOR NO WORK AT ALL?"

No. 43.
"'Grip's' Perpetual Comedy."

THE adjournment of the Ontario Legislature was immediately followed by the assembling of the Dominion Parliament at Ottawa.

March 28th, 1874.

"GRIP'S" PERPETUAL COMEDY.

"THEY HAVE THEIR EXITS AND THEIR ENTRANCES."—SHAKESPEARE.

No. 44.
"The Vacant Chair."

LOUIS RIEL, the leader of the Red River Rebellion and alleged murderer of Thomas Scott, had been returned for Provencher, Manitoba, to the Dominion Parliament. He prudently failed to take his seat in the House, while the unanimity with which both sides cried for his arrest made "the vacant chair" a bond of union for the time being.

April 4th, 1874.

THE VACANT CHAIR.
A *RIEL* BOND OF UNION.

No. 45.

"*The Science of Cheek.*"

A GREAT sensation was caused throughout the country at the announcement that Riel had actually appeared in the House at Ottawa and signed the Members' Roll. This he did *incog.*, and immediately afterwards disappeared. The cartoon anticipated his next step in the "Science of Cheek."

April 11th, 1874.

THE SCIENCE OF CHEEK;
OR, RIEL'S NEXT MOVE.

RIEL (*loq.*)—"FIVE TOUSSAND DOLLARES! BY GAR, I SHALL ARREST ZE SCOUNDREL MYSELF!"

No. 46.

"*A Touching Appeal.*"

ON the accession of Mr. Mackenzie's Government a large deficit in the treasury was discovered. Mr. Cartwright, Finance Minister, in his Budget speech, attributed this to the extravagance and corruption of the preceding administration. A new tariff was issued, in which the duties on various articles were raised considerably.

April 18th, 1874.

A TOUCHING APPEAL.
("TOUCHING" THE SECRET OF INCREASED TAXATION.)

YOUNG CANADA—"SAY, UNCLE JOHN, WON'T YOU GIVE *ME* A 'DEFICIT'? MA SAYS YOU GAVE THE GRITS ONE!"

No. 47.

"*Protestantism at Ottawa.*"

THE new tariff proved very unpopular in many points, and the Finance Minister was for several weeks fairly besieged by the representatives of various branches of trade and commerce, who called to *protest* against the objectionable items.

April 25th, 1874.

PROTESTANTISM AT OTTAWA;
OR, "JOB" CARTWRIGHT'S COMFORTERS.
BEING ONE OF THE "PLEASANTRIES OF PUBLIC LIFE."

No. 48.

"*Mrs. Gamp's Home-Thrust.*"

EARLY in the session a committee was appointed to inquire into the cause of the North-West difficulties, and during the progress of the inquiry evidence was elicited (mainly from Archbishop Tache) which implicated Sir John A. Macdonald. The Reform Party is represented in the cartoon as facetiously anticipating a repetition of the right hon. gentleman's famous asseveration of his innocence. (See Cartoon No. 11.)

MAY 2nd, 1874.

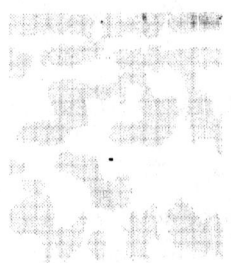

MRS. GAMP'S HOME-THRUST.

SAIREY GAMP *(The Reform Party)*—"'AVEN'T GOT NOTHINK TO SAY ABOUT THEM 'ANDS THIS TIME, I SUPPOGE, MISTER SIR JOHN!"

No. 49.

"*The Political Atlas.*"

Hon. J. R. Cartwright, Finance Minister, became the object of incessant newspaper attack. Sir Francis Hincks, who boasted a great reputation as a financier, wrote a profound essay in *The Mail* to prove Cartwright's incapacity.

May 9th, 1874.

THE POLITICAL ATLAS.
WHO WOULDN'T BE FINANCE MINISTER?

No. 50.

"*Pacific Pastimes.*"

THE Reform Government took up the Pacific Railway scheme, but initiated a new policy with regard to it. Sir John Macdonald had pledged the country to complete the entire work within ten years. Mr. Mackenzie characterized this as a physical impossibility, and proposed, as the cartoon has it, "to tak the distance in sensible like jumps, ye ken!"

MAY 16th, 1874.

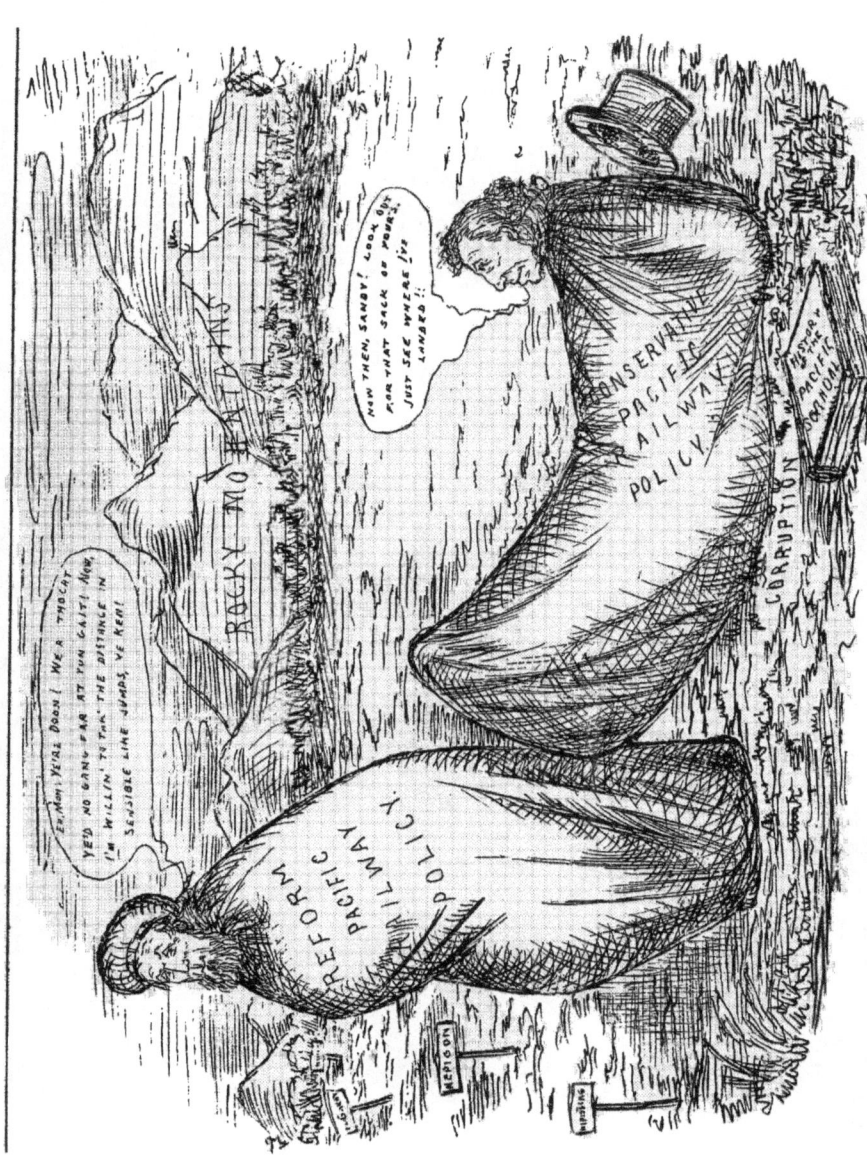

PACIFIC PASTIMES; OR, THE "HARD ROAD TO TRAVEL."

No. 51.

"*Dignity*" *without* "*Impudence.*"

The Dominion Senate, usually so passive and quiet, strikingly signalized its life and vim during this session by throwing out a bill introduced by Mr. Cameron, M.P. for South Huron, having for its object the re-distribution of the electoral divisions composing that Riding.

May 23rd, 1874.

"DIGNITY," WITHOUT "IMPUDENCE."

Old Madame Senate—"I SAY, MR. LOWER-HOUSE MACKENZIE, WHO'S RUNNING THIS COUNTRY, ANYHOW?"

No. 52.

"Ambition's Thorny Path."

Dr. John Herbert Sangster appeared as a candidate for a seat in the Council of Public Instruction. His candidature was warmly supported by many of the public school teachers of Ontario, and as ardently opposed, on personal grounds, by *The Globe* newspaper and many others.

May 23rd, 1874.

AMBITION'S THORNY PATH.

www.ingramcontent.com/pod-product-compliance
Lightning Source LLC
Chambersburg PA
CBHW020901230426
43666CB00008B/1263